SIBERIA (RUSSIA)

SIBERIA

MONGOLIA

Manzhouli

Yichun

HEILONGJIANG

Dong Uqi

Shenyang

INNER MONGOLIA

LIAONING

NORTH KOREA

Great Wall

Beijing

HEBEI

Big Fish Island

SOUTH KOREA

SHANDONG

JAPAN

Baoji

JIANGSU

SHAANXI

HUBEI

Shanghai

Anlu

Hangzhou

ZHEJIANG

YUNNAN

GUANGZHOU

TAIWAN

Lancan

Shengzhen

BURMA

VIETNAM

HONG KONG

LAOS

HAINAN

A Little Tiger

In the Chinese Night

I would like to dedicate this book to all my friends who gave me their sincere help.

© 1993 Song Nan Zhang

Published in Canada by Tundra Books, Montreal, Quebec H3Z 2N2

Published in the United States by Tundra Books of Northern New York, Plattsburgh, N.Y. 12901

Library of Congress Catalog Number: 93-60336

Canadian Cataloging in Publication Data

Zhang, Song Nan
      A little tiger in the Chinese night.
ISBN 0-88776-320-0

  1. Zhang, Song Nan—Juvenile literature. 2. Painters—Quebec (Province) — Biography — Juvenile literature. 3. Painters — China — Biography — Juvenile Literature. I. Title.

ND249.S6415A2 1993   j759.11   C93-090204-1

The publisher has applied funds from its Canada Council block grant for 1993 toward the editing and production of this book.

Design by Dan O'Leary

Printed in Hong Kong by South China Printing Co. Ltd.

A LITTLE TIGER
In the Chinese Night

An Autobiography in Art
SONG NAN ZHANG

TUNDRA BOOKS

I run to tell Mother: "There's a big cat outside." She screams: "That's not a cat. It's a tiger."

The little tiger I saw as a child

I was not yet three years old. My mother and I were hiding out in a cottage in the Bao-wu mountains because the Japanese had occupied Shanghai.

One day I ran into the kitchen, shouting: "Mom, Mom, there's a big cat outside!" I pointed to the grove where the bamboo grew tall and thick.

My mother came to the door and screamed: "That's not a cat. It's a tiger." She banged the gong to call for help.

Neighbors rushed in answer. It was a little tiger, and everyone shouted and made noise to chase it away. It went back into the bamboo, but the next day it was back again, sitting and staring at our house. Again it was chased away. On the third day the little tiger came back for the last time before disappearing into the bamboo jungle.

The appearances of the little tiger were much talked about in the village. It was rare to see a wild tiger then. Why did it not hurt me? Why did it keep coming back?

The elders said it was a good omen, that for a child to see a tiger was a sign of good luck, that I would have a lucky life.

I have lived for fifty years with the memory of that little tiger. I have thought of it often through the bad things and good things that happened to me, to my family and to China. Have I been lucky? I have certainly been luckier than many of my fellow Chinese.

I decided to tell and paint the story of my life to help me understand it. Is one life important out of one billion Chinese lives? It was important to me. Perhaps it will give others some insight into the human dimension of China over the past half century. For one billion lives are made up of a billion individual lives, each as important as any individual life anywhere in the world.

My happy days at Grandmother's house

In 1945, the war ended, the Japanese surrendered, and my family moved back to Shanghai.

The happiest times of my early years were spent at my grandmother's house in the country. A small creek ran in front of the house, and we could row down it to the town market where farmers gathered to sell their fruits and vegetables.

Bamboo grew behind the house. Every spring my grandmother would pick the fresh shoots, take them to the market to sell, and bring back toys. She also made a delicious stew of the shoots and homemade bacon.

Beyond the bamboo, over sloping fields, we could see sparkling green water, a lush and fragrant lotus pond. In early autumn, village girls sailed big wooden basins to collect water chestnuts and lotus roots. Water buffalo drank at the shore.

I particularly liked the frogs. All summer they croaked. Ah-gen, an older boy, once invited me to join his late night frog hunt. He threw a bamboo spear into a cluster of reeds, caught a frog, and gave it to me. I was terrified, seeing it struggling in my hand, and I let it go. The next day when I told my grandmother about it, she told me frogs were our friends and we should never hurt them.

When I was five, my parents sent me to a missionary school in Shanghai and I had less time to visit my grandmother. I took English classes. The first day I learned "boy" and "dog"; the second day, "girl" and "cat."

I loved to draw. Once my father broke a promise to take me out. I drew caricatures of him and put them up on the bathroom wall. Surprisingly, they did not make him angry. Instead, he said they were very well done. Did my ambition to become an artist date from then?

Grandma teaches me about frogs. She takes fresh bamboo shoots to sell in the market and brings back toys.

Shanghai, as I remember it

Shanghai was a booming city, the largest in China, and the biggest seaport in East Asia. Some 60,000 foreigners lived there and controlled much of the wealth of the city. They lived in luxurious compounds with their own army to protect them and gunships offshore to back up their power.

The textile industry was among the biggest, and one of the few large companies with a Chinese owner was Wing On Manufacturing where my father worked as a research engineer.

We were well-off compared with most Chinese who suffered flood, famine and disease like a recurring curse. We had a car and a three-story house in the western section of the city with such luxuries as an indoor toilet, hot water and a fridge. On the top floor were the children's rooms which I shared with my three younger sisters and my baby brother.

But our home was modest compared with that of the owner of the company where my father worked. He gave parties for the executives. One I attended was in the garden of his country house. Colorful sun umbrellas and tables with delicious snacks were set up on the lawn. My father bought me a little tailored suit, because all the guests were dressed in Western clothes. The older boys had all studied abroad. I decided I too wanted to go abroad someday.

After the party, we went shopping in the Wing On department store. I won first prize in a draw. Mother used the money to buy beautiful woolen blankets for me and my sister. Mine stayed in the family until it was taken away—but I am getting ahead of my story.

My sisters and brother attend my first art exhibit.

When our lives changed, along with China

I was seven when our lives changed. My first awareness of it was the cancellation of my English classes. The school was taken from the missionaries and put under government control.

The Communists took over Shanghai along with the rest of China in 1949, but it was only in 1956 that the plant where my father worked was nationalized. The owner moved to the British colony of Hong Kong where his company to this day is large and prosperous. Others moved to Hong Kong too, friends of my father, professionals like him, and the families of my school friends.

But not my father.

He was invited to Peking (now renamed Beijing) to work at the Institute of Textile Technology, the leading textile research center for all China. He was flattered by the invitation and anxious to take part in what he believed would make China better for all its people. He did not even mind that he would live in one room at the center, eat in the cafeteria, use a public washroom, and be separated from his family for a year.

My elementary school in Shanghai set up the "Young Pioneers." Only the best students were allowed to become members and we were given red scarves to wear. I was proud to be among the first students to get one. My teacher told us the worst people in the world were the American imperialists. She organized an art group and we painted anti-U.S. posters and cartoons. I was complimented on how good mine were. I was happy.

The following summer I joined my father in Beijing so I could start high school on time. I shared his room until the rest of the family arrived. We were then given a four-room apartment. My mother was devoted to her children and thought Beijing would give them a better start in life. We were keeping our house in Shanghai and my mother could always go back there, she thought.

I was so excited. Beijing was the capital of China, the heart of its culture, home of its emperors, with palaces, gardens, museums, the Great Wall nearby—and the huge square known as Tiananmen from which Mao Tse-tung had announced the triumph of the Communist Revolution and a new day for China on October 1, 1949.

We go shopping on Nanking Road. My sister and I get beautiful blankets. I dream of going abroad someday.

In 1949 the Communists take over. Our lives change forever. Father stays to help build the new China.

We are called to build a new country

It was the time of the Great Leap Forward. All Chinese were called on to build a new country. Everyone followed the communist dream. If we worked hard and produced lots of steel and food, we would be better off than any country in the world, even better off than the United States. All farmland in China was divided into communes where farmers would share the work and eat in community kitchens. We would not even need the family anymore. Food would be plentiful and free. No one would have to cook again. Many were throwing away their woks and pans.

In high school, we were ordered to collect old woks, pans and waste metal. Small steel furnaces were set up in many back yards and they needed waste metal to recycle. Every student was expected to find some. We searched our homes first, then the streets and lanes.

Classes were always being interrupted. Throughout China everyone was working to build the great new society and students had to help. Sometimes we worked during school hours, sometimes on Sundays, sometimes we were sent off for weeks to the countryside.

Every inch of ground had to be used. We planted wheat between the school buildings. It never grew because the earth was too hard. We took a week off school to plant trees on a mountain. I was disappointed years later to find that none of them had been allowed to grow.

I had the honor of being chosen to paint two murals, one on each side of the entrance to our school. I did a dragon representing China, carrying us forward to communism. On the dragon a laborer and a woman farmer marched, carrying a stoker and wheat triumphantly above their heads.

I was an obedient and docile student, most of the time. In China there are few flush toilets. We squat over trenches which have to be cleaned out. The excrement is used as fertilizer. In our school, students took turns cleaning out the trenches. Once, as another student and I carried two big buckets to a wheat field, we passed a classroom window. There was a strong wind and I had an idea. We put the buckets under the open window. Soon we heard mumbling inside the classroom. We quickly picked up the buckets and walked away. When we got back we found the smell inside was so strong the class had been dismissed.

At my high school in Beijing, I paint a mural showing a Chinese dragon carrying workers to communism.

I learn to work and endure

That winter I got my first taste of real work. We were all—teachers and students—sent to help build a dam at the Ming Tomb Reservoir north of Beijing. I did not carry anything above my head like the workers in the poster I had painted in high school. But I did march.

We were housed with a villager, and each morning as soon as it was light, we marched six or seven miles to the dam site, singing revolutionary songs. I still remember them:

"We are marching on the shining path, In a land of joyful youth;
We follow Chairman Mao our beloved leader, To a bright and glorious future."

Thousands of people worked on the dam. We all wore the bluish-gray or khaki uniforms that would be the standard dress of Chinese for decades. There was no big machinery. We dug the earth with shovels and carried it away in baskets. We students had never worked as laborers before. Those who dug had sores on their hands. I was assigned to carry a yoke. At first I couldn't even balance the baskets hanging from each shoulder. I must have walked back and forth a hundred times that day. My shoulders were so swollen I couldn't touch them. The next day was torture. My teacher said: "Good steel comes from the furnace, good shoulders come from practice. It's the time to test your willpower. Everybody should endure and continue."

We did endure and continue. In the evenings, when we returned exhausted, we had group meetings to talk about how much the work was improving us.

I wanted to be like everyone else. I wanted to be accepted. But because my father was an engineer, I was seen as a capitalist, a sinner. The self-criticism meetings were like religious meetings where everyone confessed sins. I had to learn to improve myself and get rid of capitalist thinking.

In the small village where we were housed, all water had to be carried from a distant well. When I was home, I had two basins, one for washing my face and the other for washing my feet. The students were told to bring their basins from home and I made the mistake of bringing both mine. The others brought only one. I was accused of being a spoiled capitalist. Such comforts could only soften the revolutionary spirit. After that I never brought an extra basin.

We help build a dam. The pads on my shoulders do not keep them from swelling under the heavy loads.

Into the dark and dust of a coal mine

In 1959 I was seventeen years old and I got great news. I had been accepted into the leading art school in China, Beijing's Central Institute of Fine Arts. Only fifteen candidates from all China were admitted to the oil painting department.

I felt I was on my way to becoming a painter. In the studio I sketched reproductions of Greek and Roman sculpture. But I spent as much time attending lectures on politics and studying Marxist theory. Two or three months a year, students were forced to become laborers or farmers so they would learn the meaning of work, the meaning of socialism.

In my first year, my art class was sent to work in a coal mine in Chengzhe west of Beijing. Our teacher said coal miners did the most difficult of all work, therefore their ideas were the most revolutionary.

We lived in a workers' dormitory, wore their coveralls and helmets. An elevator took us underground. At the entrance to a tunnel, the engineer sent us into a narrow space between two layers of coal, too small a space for a machine to get in. These were abandoned tunnels, too difficult to get at and containing too little coal for the professional miners to bother with. Some of the tunnels were so low, we worked half-kneeling and half-sitting. We scratched the coal away bit by bit, the only light coming from our helmets.

We returned to a wider tunnel to eat. Our eyes and teeth shone in the dark. That first day we laughed and made fun of each other as we ate steamed buns with our dusty hands, happy to be able to sit up comfortably and satisfy our hunger.

There were compensations. We got double food rations because the work was considered dangerous, and we did not have to attend political meetings in the evening.

We become miners. We laugh at our coal-blackened faces the first day as we eat steamed buns.

We scratch for food and other things

1960. It was only two years after the Great Leap Forward that was to feed us all, and we were close to starving.

Almost all food disappeared from the shops. Everything was rationed: rice, oil, sugar, meat, clothing—even matches and toilet paper. We were told that everyone had to tighten his belt.

That winter our class was sent to work on a commune in Hebei province. We were supposed to eat in the commune, but food was so scarce, we went out to find substitutes: rice husks, wheat bran, tree bark and apricot leaves. We minced elm bark into powder, mixed it with flour, and made noodles. The tree bark tasted okay, but the apricot leaves were terrible. We soaked them in water before cooking to try to get rid of the bitterness.

Before and after work we scratched for food. At night we scratched ourselves. We lived in the house of a commune member and slept on a bed of dry clay, seven or eight of us together. We could not keep clean and each night we picked lice off our bodies so we could get to sleep. A classmate, Ma Shupei, became the lice-picking champion; he caught one hundred and forty lice in one evening. He had a kidney problem and had to go outside to the toilet five or six times a night. It was so cold he never took off his filthy coat while he slept. We were not surprised he had so many lice.

Hawthorn trees grew in the area and the villagers sold the seeds. We were provided with haws to eat, and a basket was placed in our room for us to throw the seeds in. But the haws were so sour, we cooked them. After cooking, the seeds are useless for growing. We mixed them with the uncooked seeds so the cooked ones would not be noticed.

One student, Yeung, was so hungry he stole a carrot. When the teacher found out, he was accused during our evening group session of "lack of revolutionary zeal" and was severely criticized. He was so scared, he had a nervous breakdown and had to be sent back to Beijing.

That winter seemed very long and very cold, perhaps because I was always hungry.

Hungry, cold and dirty, at night on the commune we pick lice off our bodies so we can get to sleep.

Not for me, a fisherman's life

1962. The difficult years continued. For June and July we were sent with our teacher to work on Big Fish Island in Shandong province and experience the life of a fisherman.

The first day I was sent out on a boat to collect seaweed from an aquatic farm. It was a lovely day with a gentle breeze. I found it so romantic I started to sing.

When the boat stopped at the seaweed-growing area, it bounced around like a leaf in the wind. I stopped singing and threw up. Then my stomach started to ache and I got the runs. The fishermen let me lie down in the boat. When that didn't help, they brought me back to the beach. From then on I worked on shore, unloading baskets of fish, shrimp and crab.

We lived in a fisherman's house, where several of us shared a room. Our diet was sweet potato and fish. The fish was always boiled and tasteless without spice or sauce. I have tried to avoid eating fish ever since.

But I learned respect for the work fishermen do, how difficult and dangerous it is. The sea can seem so peaceful and run wild so suddenly. These fishermen with their small boats had no radios, no way of being warned of storms. To this day, whenever I see fish or shrimp I remember how hard it is to get one single fish and one single shrimp.

On the shore, as I waited for the boats to come in, I would be joined by wives waiting for their men to return. They looked out across the water, so anxiously. Women in China did not wear makeup through these years; it was not considered appropriate to the communist ideal. But these wives did. They put on lipstick as a way of welcoming the men home, of celebrating their safe return.

I think we students were often more of a nuisance than a help to the laborers, miners, farmers and fishermen we worked with through those years. But the work was very hard for us.

And there was worse to come.

I harvest seaweed on Big Fish Island. When the gentle sea turns rough I stop singing and throw up.

1966 to 1976—the crazy ten years of the Cultural Revolution. Can anyone describe the horrors?

In 1964 I had graduated from art school and was assigned to work at the cultural center of Chao Yang district on the outskirts of Beijing. I cycled between communes, teaching calligraphy and poster-making and helping with the harvest. In July of 1966 I was called back to the central office. All classes had stopped, from elementary schools right through the universities. Mao Tse-tung accused other Chinese leaders, the very men who had helped him build Communist China, of betraying the Revolution. He called on all young people to create "luan" or chaos. They were told to break everything old: old customs, old habits, old culture, old thoughts. They would break many lives.

Posters appeared on walls denouncing anyone with a capitalist background. Students, wearing khaki uniforms with red armbands, carried the Little Red Book of Chairman Mao, and picked up people on the street and in their homes. Public squares, classrooms and school halls became trial courts.

Even simple workers became targets. I, along with others from the center, was called to the trial of a city employee called Shi Shuan-xian. His job could not have been more modest: he collected toilet excrement. His crime? He had once been honored by President Liu Shaoqi for his devotion and high work ethic. When Liu was removed from office by Mao and sent away in disgrace to die, Shi was picked up. I watched with the crowd of shouting young people as the pathetic little man was accused, put in "the airplane position," and beaten half to death.

Some could not stand the accusations. At our center a poster went up accusing an office worker called Xian Ming of having deserted the army. He was interrogated night after night and locked in a dormitory. One night he managed to escape, went home, put on his best clothes, and returned to hang himself in the courtyard of the center.

The next morning a guard rushed into my room to wake me. I went out, took the man down from the tree, and called a doctor. But Xian was already dead. When his wife came, she asked us to give her his good clothes to keep. But nobody wanted to take them off him. Around noon, we used a pedicab to carry the body away for cremation. For a long time afterwards I could not get the image from my mind

I am called to watch while Red Guard students accuse and beat the pathetic little man nearly to death.

The shaming of my father

My father was the first in our family to be persecuted.

A letter he had received two years previously was used as evidence against him. We were not supposed to have contact with anyone outside the country. My father had helped a young cousin find work in Hong Kong through his old colleagues who now lived there. The letter of thanks from the cousin, preserved in some file all that time, was "proof" that my father was "a bourgeois capitalist" and a danger to the Revolution.

The Red Guard descended on my parents. My father's bank account was seized. The apartment where they lived was searched and everything of value taken, my mother's jewelry and even furniture. I visited my parents on a Sunday and found the mattress from their bed propped against a wall, waiting to be carted off. They would now have to sleep on hay over boards to get rid of their bourgeois habits.

I was living in one room at the cultural center and had stored all my paintings, some forty canvases, at my parents'. The Red Guard found nudes among them—the studies every art student does to learn human anatomy—and told my mother they would be back later to deal with them. In a panic she burned all my paintings.

The house they had kept in Shanghai to which my mother hoped to return someday was confiscated and the contents seized, including the blanket I had won as a child. The aunt who had been living there was given one room. Seven families were moved in.

At the textile institute, my father was demoted to sweeping the floor and cleaning the toilets. He was ordered to write a confession each day, describing a capitalist sin he had committed, and to attend self-criticism meetings. My mother was assigned to sweep the streets and alleys around where she lived. She became ill from fear and frustration and would remain an invalid for the rest of her life.

Three years later, the pursuit of my father continued. In 1969, although he was now sixty-six years old, he was sent along with other engineers and intellectuals to be "reeducated" in Hubei. There he was first assigned to boil water each morning for the residents and later to pick weeds and care for the cows.

The banishment of my sisters and brother

The persecution that began with my father now descended on my sisters and brother. One by one they were investigated and sent away.

Song Yin, the oldest of my three sisters, had graduated in forestry engineering. She was doing forestry management in Heilongjiang, near the Siberian border. When it was discovered that her father had been a capitalist, she was transferred to Yichun in the mountains to cut wood with a team of twenty men.

My middle sister, Li Yin, was studying mechanical engineering. She was sent to work in a machine-building factory in Shenyang, an industrial city in Liaoning province where she was often ill from the pollution. "My nose is black at the end of every day," she wrote me. Later she was transferred to a car manufacturing plant in the mountains.

My youngest sister, Mei Yin, was sent to Yunnan on the Burma border to cut and burn trees and cultivate a farm for quinine to be used as a medicine against malaria.

My brother, Yi Nan, was sent to the Mongolian border to live in a yurt with a nomadic family, herding sheep and horses.

I would not see any of them for seven years. In the evenings I wrote to them, realizing I was lucky to still be near Beijing. But I was under suspicion and was repeatedly called to answer accusations, sometimes by the Red Guard, sometimes by the army.

We use a pedicab to carry away the body for cremation.

My father is accused. His house, savings and furniture are confiscated. He is sent to be reeducated.

My sisters and brother are banished to the far corners of China. I will not see them for seven years.

How love found a way

The only happiness in those years was that I fell in love.

It was through my art that I met Sheng Li. I had been ordered back from the communes to the cultural center for a few months. I was still highly suspect, but they needed me. Portraits of Mao were going up all over China and there was a shortage of artists. I did so many portraits of Mao, friends joke that I can paint him with my eyes blindfolded. One of my illustrations was printed and distributed in millions of copies.

I was painting a ten-foot-high oil portrait of Mao when a girl who worked as an accountant nearby visited the studio out of curiosity. I thought she was the loveliest girl I had ever seen and I offered to do her portrait. So began our difficult courtship.

Her friends warned her against me. I had been president of the student union for two years before graduating. A poster went up asking why the son of a capitalist instead of a worker had held that honor. Fortunately, her family approved of me. But we could not get married until we found a place to live. We had trouble even finding a place to be alone to talk. In warm weather on Sundays we walked in a park, but in winter it was too cold.

After a year and a half I heard of a vacant room in a compound. I went to look at it but couldn't get in. The door was piled with garbage which dirty water had turned into an ice-mountain. I dug away the garbage and opened the door. It was as depressing inside as out. I cleaned out the dirt and spider nests. Here we set up our first home, one room with a bed, a table, some chairs and a coal stove.

To be married, we simply registered at the government office and received two certificates. Our wedding picture was an ID photograph of our two heads. In the evening, friends came and brought presents: three statuettes of Mao, two sets of his Little Red Books, and a farmer's scythe so we would never forget the ideals of the Revolution. We served candy, wine and tea.

We were happy to be together at last, but the investigations did not stop. I was always being called to answer questions about what I had said or written years before, or about other people, why I had been their friend or helped them.

At our wedding party in our one room, guests bring statues of Mao, his Little Red Books and a scythe.

The chaos finally ends

The nightmare that began in 1966 eased with the death of Mao in 1976. So much had happened.

During those first years of our marriage my wife and I were always separated. I was away six days a week, went home on Sundays, often taking an hour and a half each way by bicycle. I worked in communes all around Beijing, farming alongside the workers in the day and holding group talks at night. There are not many farm jobs I don't know. I planted and harvested rice, corn and other vegetables. I worked on construction sites, built roads and helped a veterinarian on a pig farm.

In 1970 our first son, Hao Yu, was born. In 1972 our second son, Hao Yong, arrived.

Finally, in 1978, two years after the death of Mao, the new premier, Deng Xiaoping, announced, "There will be no more chaos." The country turned in a new direction.

Everything relaxed. China opened to the world and offered new hope for the people.

During the Cultural Revolution, the only acceptable art was by peasants and workers. Professional artists like myself would now be supported by the government. I returned to the art institute on a research fellowship, and in 1980 I was appointed a teacher of mural painting.

I need teach only a few hours a week. I received important commissions, one of which was to design a mural for the National Library in Beijing. At last I could give most of my time to my art. Each holiday I managed to travel. I visited most of the provinces of China, going as far north as the Manchurian border and all the way south to Hainan Island on the South China Sea.

My wife and I found an apartment in a compound on a street called Happy Lane. We were a family of four living in three rooms and it seemed a luxury after the single room we had been in and we felt lucky.

In the compound seventeen rooms accommodated nine families. Some neighbors had three generations living in one room. No one had running water or a bathroom. A public water tap was in the middle of the courtyard and people were always fighting to get to it to do their laundry. The toilets were shared with the people from another compound next door. Every day before and after work, we lined up to use them. Sometimes they were so messy and dirty, it was unbearable to go in. They were cleaned out once or twice a week by a man who came with his wagon and horses.

The courtyard was untidy and crowded. On rainy days the lane was mud. In winter the tap froze, so the water was turned off at night. Each family had to store water. We cooked with coal cakes, and dust was everywhere.

It was a lively place. Peddlers brought fruits and vegetables from the state farms. A black marketer sold rice. The mailman arrived by bicycle. Old men played chess. Somebody was always shaking out ash so that unburned coal pieces could be reused. Babies in bamboo carriages were fed outdoors when the weather was good.

Children loved to climb on the cement tile roofs to play with the pigeons. They enjoyed themselves, but they were always breaking the tiles so the roofs leaked.

Arguments were frequent because so many lived in such a small area. But in an emergency, we all helped each other.

Happy Lane would be our family home for fourteen years.

My wife lights a fire in the coal stove in our flat.

In Happy Lane, our family of four finds a three-room apartment (second from left, backyard is visible).

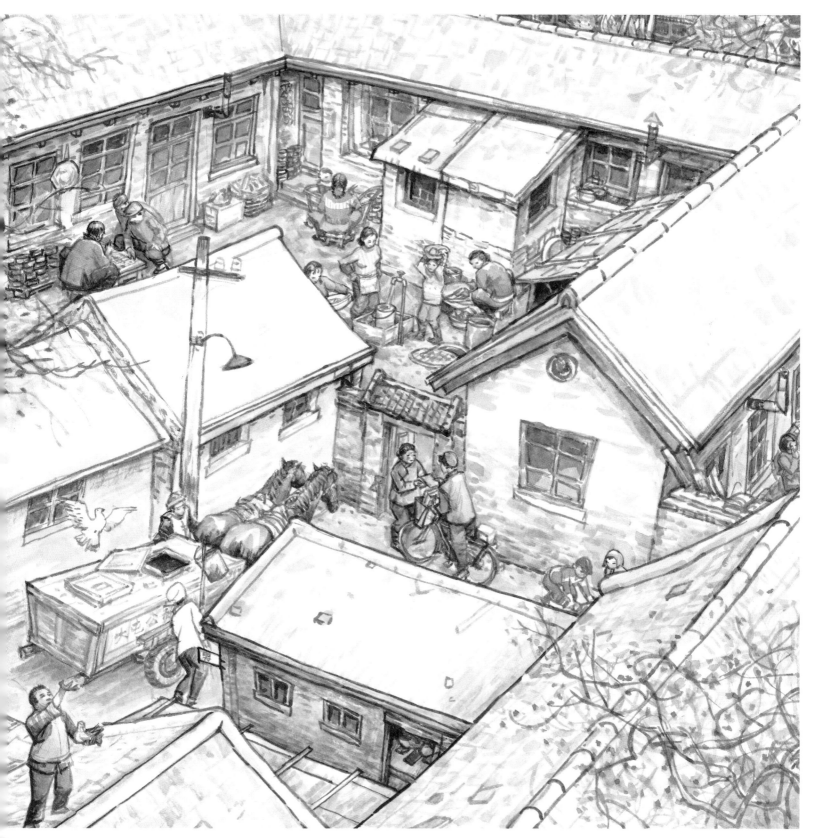

We fight to wash clothes and line up for the toilets which are shoveled out into a cart drawn by horses.

The shock of seeing France

In 1984 something wonderful happened. I was chosen to go to France as an exchange student. I was no longer young but the dream of going abroad I had since childhood was to be realized.

France was a shock to me. For decades I had been told that in capitalist countries only a few were rich and everyone else was poor. I discovered that everything I had been told, everything I had believed, was a lie.

We foreign students were sent first to Vichy for lessons in French language and culture. Two evenings after my arrival, as I walked around with other Chinese students, we passed an art studio and decided to enter. We were graciously received and one of the painters invited us to his home. He turned out to be a clerk in the post office who painted in the evenings. His home astonished me. Here was a man in a modest job who could support a family, have his own house and garden, a car, and the time and money to paint as a hobby.

Of all the students I met from nineteen other countries, we Chinese were the poorest. When we were invited to join others for coffee, we had to refuse because we did not have money to pay for it. Nevertheless, by shopping for the cheapest food and eating in my room, I managed to save enough to visit other European cities. Everywhere ordinary people were rich by Chinese standards.

Paris was particularly wonderful, but shortly after arriving there I got a frightening letter from my wife. She and my sons had nearly been killed. One snowy night, the chimney in our little flat in Happy Lane got blocked and toxic gas came back into the rooms. Hao Yu, my older son, arrived home to find his mother and brother passed out from the fumes. He roused them just in time and got help. Neighbors took them to the hospital. I was so distressed to think I might have lost them and so relieved to know they were all right, I went to Notre-Dame Cathedral and lit a candle. I am not religious, but I wanted to do something to show my gratitude.

I loved Paris. One day in the Rodin Museum I watched a child sketching in front of a sculpture. I envied him so much I photographed the scene. He was so young and already he was allowed into museums on his own. I was forty-three and I was seeing these masterpieces for the first time.

In the Rodin Museum in Paris I see a child sketching. How lucky he seems compared with Chinese children.

Back to China and the "real" world

In 1985 I came back from Paris, inspired and full of enthusiasm to paint. China was even more open to the world than when I had left. Foreigners were welcome. Thousands of Americans were teaching all over the country. Everyone was hopeful. I was forty-four and I had been wanting to become a painter for thirty years. But how little of that time I had spent painting. The political struggles in China had taken away my youthful years.

Now other problems interfered. "You are very lucky," my wife reminded me. "You have had a chance to see the world. Now you are back in the real world." She did not need to remind me. The real world was all around us in our small house filled with dust when the wind blew in the intense heat of the Beijing summer, where water dripped through the roof when it rained, where we had to clean out the coal ash in winter and line up for the toilets all year.

At the art institute, I was made assistant director. This was supposed to be an honor, but it consumed my days. In China, universities are responsible for every aspect of student lives, not just classes, but sleeping quarters, meals and health. I also had to look after the staff and their housing, family planning, births and deaths. I was trapped in never-ending office work.

At home we had another problem. My mother had been ill for twenty years, ever since the Red Guard attack on her home. Now an operation for a tumor on her brain left her half-paralysed, blind in one eye, and unable to speak. We brought her to live with us, set up a bed by the window in my sons' room, and we all took turns caring for her.

I carry my mother from the hospital to live with us.

Where Marco Polo walked

In 1987, after two years of administrative work, I managed to switch to a teaching job that would leave me time to paint and I made the last of my big trips in China. What a trip it was! In all China, Xinjiang province in the northwest was the most difficult to get to and the area I most wanted to see.

Here the snowcapped mountains tower over a vast plateau of desert and grasslands. People live much as they did when Marco Polo crossed it on the Silk Road from Italy to Peking 700 years ago. We traveled on an old bus that kept breaking down and we slept in government hostels. But such inconveniences were minor in return for what we saw as we circled the Gobi desert from the northern capital of Urumqi to Tash Qurghan near the border of Pakistan, then to Hotan in the desert.

The people are of mixed race and religion, reflecting the waves of immigration over the centuries.

In the north the Weiwer people speak Turkish and live in villages where much is made of the fine grapes and beautiful women. "When the grapes ripen, they intoxicate the hearts of young girls." They also grow the finest watermelon in the world, a gourmet fruit that we never saw in Beijing, but brings high prices in Hong Kong. It is so sweet and cool you should eat it, they say, seated in front of the fire in the evenings.

In the grasslands surrounding the desert, nomads still herd sheep and live in clay huts and tents. The Tibetan yak, protected by its long hair against the cold, provides milk and meat for food, skins for warmth and hide for drums to accompany singing and dancing. Two-humped camels are still used for transport, their hair for weaving and their turds for fuel.

I returned home to paint ten large canvases for an exhibition. Four were sold to an American businessman. With the money I decided to go abroad again, this time to Canada. Friends I had met at the Canadian Embassy found me an inexpensive flat in Montreal.

It was there I experienced the tragedy of Tiananmen Square.

In China I most wanted to see Xinjiang where the colorful dress reflects the many races and religions.

Goats, yaks and two-humped camels support age-old nomadic life in the grasslands at the desert edge.

Tiananmen—and a new horror

For two months in the spring of 1989, alone in that little Montreal flat, I watched on a black-and-white TV screen the happenings at Tiananmen Square.

I followed the news, from the first small student demonstrations that asked only for reform. Corruption was rife among the upper echelons of the Communist Party. They were known to make lavish visits to Hong Kong. At the same time inflation had increased sixty percent. People were hoarding whatever they could buy because their money would be worth less the next week.

The signal for the first demonstration was the death of Hu Yaobang. He had been dismissed as secretary-general of the Communist Party two years earlier because he had supported students asking for more democracy for China. He was known as an honest leader, against the corruption. In dying, he became the rallying point.

The students were condemned as troublemakers and told to go back to their classes. Instead, they went on a hunger strike and were joined by workers and farmers. On May 15th, a million people gathered in the rain in Tiananmen Square. Now they wanted more than reform; they wanted democracy.

As the statue of the Goddess of Democracy and Freedom went up, my eyes were glued to the TV set. The statue had been built in my school, the Central Institute of Fine Arts. I recognized the faces of students I knew in the crowd.

Then, in horror and disbelief, in the days that followed I saw the soldiers arrive and the tanks move in to carry out the massacre of hundreds of students.

What was happening to my wife and sons? What was happening to China? I was frantic.

Finally, my wife was able to get to a phone and call me. Knowing how worried I must be, she braved going out in the curfew where anyone seen was shot, in order to give me news. My family was safe, but under no circumstances should I return to China. I must try to get them to Canada.

What I did not know, what my wife had kept from me in order not to worry me, what she told me only then, was that for two months my older son, Hao Yu, had been among the students who occupied Tiananmen Square.

In a flat in Montreal, I watch helpless as the army and tanks spread terror in Tiananmen Square.

Getting my family out of China

For two days after the massacre at Tiananmen Square I stayed in my flat, weeping. I worried about my family, I grieved for the students killed, and I despaired for China.

Then began my efforts to get my family to Canada. I was particularly worried about Hao Yu. Would he be arrested along with other students who were being hunted and picked up? What would happen when he tried to leave the country?

The Canadian government immediately gave me a special permit to stay in Canada. But it took me more than a year to get the documents required by the Canadian immigration department for the family to come. I had sold a few paintings, earning enough to live on, but I did not have money for the expensive legal help that might have speeded up the process.

The Canadian bureaucracy was gentle compared with what my wife and sons went through to get out of China. They needed passports to leave. Hao Yu stood in line all one cold winter night —he says it was the coldest night he ever spent— just to get into the passport office. Then he was interrogated for hours.

"They knew everything about me," he says. "Everything I had said and done in school. They knew I had skipped school six years before to go swimming, that I had once been in a fight with another student. I got the impression they had a file on everyone in China. It was useless to say I had not been in Tiananmen Square. They knew I had. What saved me was that my face had not appeared on any of the TV screens." Finally, after four months, my wife and sons got their passports to leave.

Then came the application for Canadian visas. For that Hao Yu and my younger son lined up for seven days and nights outside the Canadian embassy. "At least it was summer," he remembers, "but it was still exhausting. Thousands of people were trying to get out of China. Hao Yong and I took shifts to keep our place in line."

My fiftieth birthday—a celebration.

At last, a year and a half after Tiananmen Square, my wife and sons arrived in Canada. Need I describe my joy as I greeted them at the Montreal airport?

My fiftieth birthday was a great moment for celebrating with the Canadian friends who had helped me. I looked at my sons. They are both in college in Montreal. How different from my own youth! My wife is studying French and English. I notice her makeup and her dress. She wears only bright colors now.

What can I say about my life? Did the little tiger bring me luck?

My luck seems to have come and gone, just as the little tiger came and went. At present I feel very lucky indeed.

But what happened to the little tiger itself? Did it find a place to live and grow without being chased back into the dark?

Will the people of China ever find such a place?

I welcome my wife and sons as they arrive in Montreal

Together at last with my wife and sons, we celebrate my fiftieth birthday with Canadian friends in Montreal.

My sons are in college. My wife studies. I paint every day. Did that little tiger bring me luck after all?

HISTORICAL BACKGROUND

China is one of the oldest civilizations in the world, dating back more than 4,000 years.

The Chinese live in a land blessed with stunning environmental diversity and rich in natural resources. By the time Marco Polo visited China in the 1200s, it had been the center of East Asian civilization for more than two thousand years. The Chinese were far more technologically advanced than the Europeans, having already invented paper and printing, porcelain, gunpowder and silk, and their population was far greater, their cities vibrant with culture and commerce. For this reason, Europeans had a hard time believing the fantastic stories Marco Polo told upon his return. The Great Wall of China, first constructed in the third century BC, was built to keep northern nomadic "barbarians" from attacking the communities of north China and to protect the Silk Road trade route to the West opened up by Chinese and Central Asian merchants. By the 1700s, China was economically self-sufficient and emerging faster from a worldwide recession than any other country, while the West was quickly advancing in science and technology following the discoveries of the Scientific Revolution. Westerners kept pouring huge amounts of silver into China to pay for the luxuries of tea, porcelain and silk, which were being traded through a monopoly in Canton established by the Chinese emperor. As a result, the Westerners were saddled with a massive trade deficit. The only product they could find that the Chinese people were interested in was opium, a highly addictive drug that comes from the poppy plant. Although the Chinese government had banned the importation of opium, the British, and then the Americans and Dutch, illegally traded with Chinese entrepreneurs. Gradually, millions of people living in the southern parts of China became addicted. Law and order began to break down and the society began to collapse.

1835 - The Chinese react by closing their ports to the opium trade. This angers the British.

1839-1842 - The First Opium War. The British Navy, the strongest in the world at the time, bombards the Chinese coast. The British win the war and sign the Treaty of Nanking. The Chinese are forced to open up more coastal cities as treaty ports with Europeans. Britain is also granted an island called Hong Kong.

1894-95 - More foreign countries control parts of China: France, Germany, Russia, Britain, Japan and the United States. The Chinese worry that their country is being "carved up like a melon." The Japanese and China fight a war over Korea and Formosa (Taiwan). The Japanese win.

1900 - The Boxer Rebellion. Based in the northeast, a coalition of secret societies, objecting to the demands of Western missionaries and the collapse of the national economy, attacks foreigners throughout China, culminating in an assault on the foreign embassies in Peking (Beijing). This last attack is put down by foreign troops who then loot the Forbidden City, the ceremonial heart of China. Western governments impose an enormous fine on China, increasing the country's financial problems dramatically.

1911 - Sun Yat-sen leads the Nationalist revolution against the Qing dynasty and establishes the Republic of China.

1919 May 4 - Students demonstrate in Beijing against concessions given the Japanese at the Versailles Peace Conference in Europe and its growing influence on the Chinese government. The protests are so widespread they change the political and cultural policies of the government and the attitude of the Chinese people. Called the May 4th Movement.

1921 - The Communist Party of China founded in Shanghai.

1925 - Sun Yat-sen dies.

1927 - The ruling Nationalist Party of Chiang Kai-shek attacks the Communists, who have grown popular in many parts of China, starting a civil war.

1931 - The Japanese take control of Manchuria and rename it Manchuko.

1934-35 - The Long March. The Communists retreat over a 6,000 mile route, from Jiangxi in the southeast to Shaanxi in the northwest. During the 370 days of the march they spread their message, winning sympathizers in the countryside. During the course of the March, Mao Tse-tung takes over the leadership of the Communist Party.

1937 - The Communists and Nationalists stop fighting each other to battle the Japanese, who are now attacking cities in southern China, including Shanghai and Nanking. The Japanese occupy many of these cities, including Shanghai, for the next seven years.

1945 - World War II ends. The Japanese are driven out of China. Another civil war breaks out between the Nationalists and the Communists.

1949 - The Nationalist Party flees to Taiwan, a large island off the coast of China. Mao Tse-tung, Chairman of the Communist Party, announces the formation of the People's Republic of China from Tiananmen Square, Beijing, on October 1.

1949-50 - The Communists persecute people they think are "counter-revolutionaries" —landlords, wealthy merchants, Nationalist sympathizers and criminals.

1958-61 - The government decides that the country can become modern very quickly if everyone gets involved and announces a plan called the Great Leap Forward. Communes are set up across the country and private property is confiscated. Millions of people are organized to build large projects like dams. Students are sent to the countryside to help farmers. But because of bad agricultural policies, famine results in large areas of the countryside.

1962 - Socialist Education Movement. Thousands of (Communist) Party workers and "ex-capitalists" are sent to the countryside to be "educated" by farmer groups.

1966 - Start of the Cultural Revolution. Mao decides to "purify" the country and the revolution and weed out those people he believes are not following the communist path. He creates the Red Guards, an army of "ideologically sound" young people from "good" families (workers, farmers, army, party members) to make sure that people are thinking properly.

1967 - Three hundred and fifty million copies of Mao's Little Red Book are published. A small book of the Chairman's sayings, it is memorized by Red Guard members and millions of others. The Red Guard goes on a nationwide rampage of destruction, abuse and persecution. Millions of people are publicly humiliated, tortured and driven to suicide. Old temples, schools and monuments are destroyed.

1968 - Mao is forced to disband the Red Guard. Many are sent to the countryside to be "reeducated." This results in a generation of people who are deeply resentful of the government and its policies. The Cultural Revolution is beginning to be seen as a failure.

1972 - American President Richard Nixon visits China and diplomatic and cultural relations are resumed. China starts opening up to the world again.

1976 - The Premier of China, Chou En-lai, dies. In April thousands of people gather in Tiananmen Square to mourn his death and to protest Mao's policies and the Cultural Revolution. The police attack the Square and hundreds of people are killed. In September Chairman Mao dies. A power struggle takes place in the party. Maoists in the party are purged and the "Gang of Four," including Mao's widow, are put on trial, blamed for the ills of the country and the excesses of the Cultural Revolution.

1978 - China and Japan sign a treaty of peace and friendship.

1980 - The Premier, Deng Xiaoping, allows more freedom for artists and religions. He also allows a controlled amount of free enterprise, especially in the southern parts of the country.

1985 - There are more than nine million private businesses in China.

1987 - Reform-minded party officials take control and capitalism grows. The Chinese economy becomes one of the fastest growing in the world.

1989 - The economy continues to grow, causing high inflation. In March students in Beijing first demonstrate against inflation and corruption among government officials, then demand free speech and reform. April 20 - Deng Xiaoping criticizes the students, saying the country will head toward "chaos." Protests grow and move to Tiananmen Square. May 4 - The seventieth anniversary of the May 4th Movement. Workers from the Beijing area join the students. May 13 - Students start a hunger strike to pressure the government. May 15 - Soviet President Mikhail Gorbachev visits Beijing and is cheered by the students. May 18 - One million people go to the Square to support the hunger strikers. May 21 - The government declares martial law in Beijing. The army is called in and surrounds the city. May 22 - June 4 - Citizens block all major roads, trains and subways leading to the center of the city, making sure the army cannot get to the Square. Millions come to Beijing from all parts of China to support the demonstration. The media help spread the ideas of the protesters throughout China. May 30 - Students from the Beijing Art Institute bring their Goddess of Democracy statue to the Square. June 4 - At midnight power is turned off and all lights go out in central Beijing, allowing the army to move in. 1:00 AM - The lights return. Thousands of soldiers surround Tiananmen Square. They enter, first firing tear gas and then live bullets. Hundreds of people are killed. This is the first time that the Chinese army has fired on its own people. July - Student leaders are arrested. Others go into hiding or leave the country.

1990 to the present - China has the fastest growing economy in the world. The country adopts a combination of communism and the free market that allows for growth and the creation of a middle-class. Western companies pour into China, seeing it as the largest untapped market in the world.

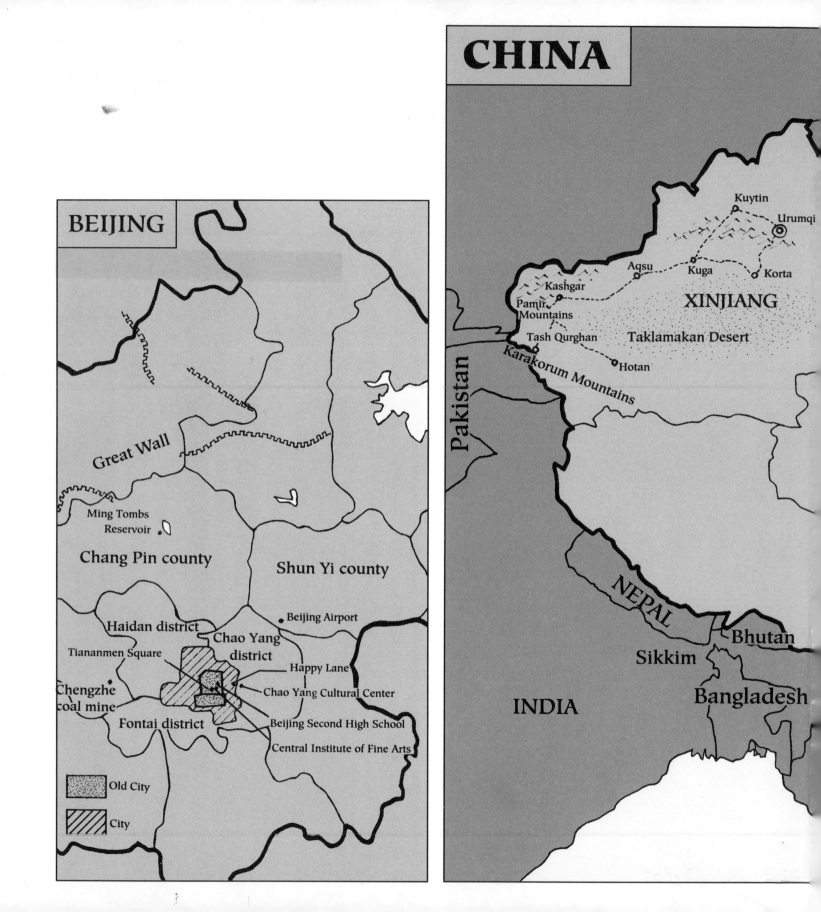

BEIJING

Great Wall

Ming Tombs
Reservoir

Chang Pin county

Shun Yi county

Haidan district

Chao Yang
district

Tiananmen Square

Beijing Airport

Happy Lane

Chao Yang Cultural Center

Chengzhe
coal mine

Central Institute of Fine Arts

Beijing Second High School

Fontai district

Old City

City

CHINA

Kuytin

Urumqi

Aqsu

Kuga

Korta

Kashgar

XINJIANG

Pamir
Mountains

Tash Qurghan

Taklamakan Desert

Karakorum Mountains

Hotan

Pakistan

NEPAL

Bhutan

Sikkim

INDIA

Bangladesh